# Half Full, Half Empty, or Just a Glass of Unpredictable Life

*poems by*

# Harold Whisman

*Finishing Line Press*
Georgetown, Kentucky

# Half Full, Half Empty, or Just a Glass of Unpredictable Life

*For Cathy, Sarah, Jason, Adam, Harrison, Ina, and Kim
who always make my glass half full*

Copyright © 2024 by Harold Whisman
ISBN 979-8-88838-725-2 First Edition
All rights reserved under International and Pan-American Copyright Conventions. No part of this book may be reproduced in any manner whatsoever without written permission from the publisher, except in the case of brief quotations embodied in critical articles and reviews.

ACKNOWLEDGMENTS

My thanks to the editors of the following publications in which the listed poem previously appeared, some in slightly different form:

*Amethyst*: "Pulling Weeds from the Cracks in My Brick Sidewalk"
*Ancient Paths*: "The Daisies at Our House"
*Better than Starbucks*: "Haikus 1, 7, and 10," "Cutting Back," and "Sneaky Squirrels"
Poetry Nation's Anthology *Turning the Corner: Milestone*: "Winter Storm"
*Smoky Blue Literary and Arts Magazine*: "The Prognosticator's Vision"


Publisher: Leah Huete de Maines
Editor: Christen Kincaid
Cover Art: Sarah Whisman
Author Photo: Kim Moore
Cover Design: Elizabeth Maines McCleavy


Order online: www.finishinglinepress.com
also available on amazon.com

Author inquiries and mail orders:
Finishing Line Press
PO Box 1626
Georgetown, Kentucky 40324
USA

# Contents

## I. HALF FULL

The Sign .................................................................................................. 2
Everbody Has a C .................................................................................. 4
Snapshots of My Father, Number 1 ..................................................... 5
Haikus, First Grouping .......................................................................... 6
The Daisies at Our House ..................................................................... 7
The Jester ................................................................................................ 8
Thanksgiving Lawn Display ................................................................. 9
Snapshots of My Father, Number 2 ................................................... 10

## II. HALF EMPTY

Winter Storm ....................................................................................... 12
Late October ........................................................................................ 13
Puppy at the Animal Shelter .............................................................. 14
Trash ..................................................................................................... 15
Haikus, Second Grouping .................................................................. 16
Snapshots of My Father, Number 3 ................................................... 17
Visiting a Longtime Friend ................................................................ 18
Bad Karma ........................................................................................... 20
The Prognosticator's Vision ............................................................... 21

## III. JUST A GLASS OF UNPREDICTABLE LIFE

The Thing about Love ........................................................................ 24
Pulling Weeds from the Cracks in My Brick Sidewalk ................... 25
Cutting Back ........................................................................................ 27
Haikus, Third Grouping ..................................................................... 28
Something Unexpected ...................................................................... 29
Sneaky Squirrels .................................................................................. 31
Snapshots of My Father, Number 4 ................................................... 32
What Matters Most ............................................................................. 34

# I. HALF FULL

## THE SIGN
*Dedicated to Cathy, my wife of 52 years*

Young *GQ*-armored knights dismount from chrome horses
and enter a neon-lit castle crowded with ladies in waiting.

Inside, under a pale pulsating glow where the four enchanted elves'
mesmerizing sounds bounce off shadows full of frenzied motion,
these knights and ladies pair off in a custom as old as the coming of
  spring.
Then they bounce and bop, swing and shimmy, twist and twirl in the
  ecstasy of *you* and *me*.

Your auburn hair flies gently about in the air-conditioned breeze,
spilling softly over your shoulders and flowing down
until it reaches the depths of your lower back,
beauty that attracts the eye as a melodious song attracts the ear.

Outside, in every direction these knights and ladies turn,
stands a wicked and warped forest, whose magical herbs
and twisted paths offer neither solace nor escape.
I ask, "Who will rescue me from this wilderness?"

You take my hand and laugh with the joy of a young child,
and a smile remains that flashes into my consciousness
like the sun when it first rises over a distant hilltop,
remains upon a face of smoothness and delight
with bright, beautiful, bewitching eyes of green
and a cover girl's nose centered above lush coral lips.
You answer, "Those who are worthy of rescue must search for a sign."

I ask, "How can I find a sign in these woods so dark and dangerous?"
Your smile fades into a frown.
You answer with a question, "Are you not an apprentice knight?"
"Yes, I am an apprentice knight."
"Am I not the lady you seek to serve?"
"Yes, you are she."
"Then look into your heart. It holds the only sign you need."

So I search my heart as thoroughly as a family searches its home for a
  missing heirloom
until deep within one of its chambers I find a hidden yellow box.
This box holds a sign that unfolds to read:

*Sharing*

       *love*

           *is*

              *the*

                  *answer.*

Warm hands clasp.
Warm lips touch.
Warm bodies caress.
I dream as kings do and as kings know not how.

I pray these dreams never die.
You now pray at my side.

## EVERYBODY HAS A C

Once in a youthful dream, no doubt *Playboy* influenced, I saw a street full of nude women. Noticeably attractive were many, yet many were not, much the same as in one's waking life. Endlessly they paraded by, heading to work or a gym or shops or even playgrounds with small children in tow. This strange spectacle I watched, completely enthralled as though I were watching the latest summer blockbuster film. Red-wine hair, long and lustrous, was the first thing I noticed when she appeared. Unlike all the others she was fully clothed was the second thing. Erotically so (her being clothed) was the third thing, in a stylish black dress that subtly suggested the delightful treasures hidden underneath. Looking a thousand times more beautiful and a thousand times more interesting than any of the unclothed women in my dream, she walked to the middle of this street, stopped, and turned her head to stare directly at me. On cue she spoke seductively as her eyes gazed into my soul. Vaguely, I heard someone say her name, but I only caught that it began with a C, for soon I could hear or see nothing except this voluptuous vision dressed in black. Easily as Cupid lifts his bow, she lifted my heart forever from its fancied resting place.

## SNAPSHOTS OF MY FATHER, NUMBER 1

My father looked comical
dressed in his postal outfit,
appearing ready to make
deliveries, but the beaming
smile brightening his whole
face had nothing to do with
his lack of appropriate attire.

He was beaming because he
was looking at his firstborn
child, a son, whom he cradled
somewhat awkwardly in his
arms as if he were unsure
how to handle this fragile
package. That child was me.

My father stared down
at this miraculous creation
for a long time, his smile
never fading. Every once
in a while he would glance
at my mother, who also had
a smile but on a fatigued face.

It is hard to know what he
was thinking, but I imagine
he felt like a man who had
just hit life's jackpot. Five
years earlier he had been
fighting against the Japanese
in life-and-death skirmishes.

Still smiling, my father bent
down and kissed my mother
on the forehead before handing
the baby back to her. Then he
left the room, walking out into
a world as full of possibilities
as the Milky Way is of stars.

## HAIKUS, FIRST GROUPING

1.
Surrounded by drab,
near lifeless green, a bright red
bloom springs forth, smiling.

2.
A gentle salty
breeze moves to the rhythmic beat
of the soaring waves.

3.
A rainbow vintage—
autumn foliage aged to
brilliant perfection.

4.
Giant white flakes fall.
Youthful laughter can be heard
on nearby hilltops.

**THE DAISIES AT OUR HOUSE**

After a harsh winter
filled with arctic winds

numbing our fingers
and faces, after the same

winter gave life-altering
birth to a new pandemic

forcing us into semi-isolation,
the daisies at our house

flourished in the spring,
giving us big golden winks,

as if to say, hang in there
because beauty and grace

are still here
and always will be.

## THE JESTER

My daughter Sarah, the artist,
is one of six significant
women in my life. In college
she painted herself looking like
a jester for a self-portrait.

She was hinting at her sharp wit
since she plays the fool for no one.
Her banter makes me laugh even
when she says gremlins must sneak in
nightly and sew my clothes tighter.

Her employer looks at her web—
design skills and chuckles over
his good fortune (and probably
at her jokes, too). She earns almost
double what I did in a year.

As a mother, she reminds me
of a favorite teacher—
loving, patient, and involved.
She gives her children laughter,
hugs, fun horseplay, and sound guidance.

Whenever my thoughts turn to her
or she shows up at my house,
a faint smile dances across
my face, but a much bigger
smile dances across my heart.

## THANKSGIVING LAWN DISPLAY

My wife and I have a Thanksgiving lawn display,
an inflatable of a turkey wearing a Pilgrim hat,
that we always put out after Halloween.
For several previous Novembers,
he was always alone on our front lawn,
being blown about by the wind like a garden flag
and battered by the rain like a fragile flower.
This November we placed him next to our house
between a pyracantha and an azalea bush.
These two bushes, along with the house, provide protection
from the elements for poor Tom (the name we call him).
Both bushes also provide him companionship,
for his face glows a bit brighter since the move.
Whenever I walk by them during the day,
I swear I can hear them whispering to each other.
They are likely complaining about changes in the weather
or gossiping about the tumultuous lives of their owners.
No matter what the conversation may be, Tom
always sounds cheerful. He must believe
friends make the world a better place.

## SNAPSHOTS OF MY FATHER, NUMBER 2

Sunday: My father took our family
on a scenic drive to western North
Carolina for a delicious homestyle
country meal (fried chicken, mashed
potatoes with gravy, an array of fresh
fruits and vegetables, and so many
tempting pies). My father hummed
along to a radio tune as he drove
with my mother sitting close to him
and my sister and I playing road games
in the back seat (my arm sore since
she always won at "Punch Bug").
After dinner we rode on the popular
Tweetsie Railroad (I enjoyed the train
robbery the most). We also stopped to
get mineral water from a natural spring.

The trip back to our home in a small
southwest Virginia valley seemed
longer, and I nearly fell asleep.
My father still hummed as he drove.
When we entered the valley where
we lived, we passed Dickey's Knob,
a peak standing tall like an imposing
guard at the valley's eastern entrance.
My father and I once hiked to the top
of this peak, where we discovered, as
if we were at a lookout, a spectacular
view of our farming community and
the peaceful mountains surrounding it.

Later that evening we all watched
*The Ed Sullivan Show*. My father
laughed so hard at the comedian
on the show his eyes became as moist
as early morning grass, his face looked
sunburnt, and he tilted forward, nearly
slipping off the living room couch. I don't
remember ever hearing him laugh any louder.
It was a perfect end to a pleasant day.

# II. HALF EMPTY

## WINTER STORM

The snow starts slowly with large and lovely flakes
that flutter like a lover's hands in moonlight,
but soon the flakes are coming thick and quite fast
like breath from someone caught in passion's own storm.

The snow continues through the day, coming down
so hard we can't see the white fence fifty feet
from our back door. By nightfall it's official—
a blizzard—and inside our house it's the same.

When I attempt to wrap my arms around Blake,
she pulls away. When I attempt to kiss her,
she turns away. Her black eyes grow icy. I feel
as lost as a man holding a map he can't read.

By the next morning the snow has covered all,
forcing the world within to unfurl a white flag.
Waist-deep, the snow won't allow anyone to go forward
or turn back. And spring is months, maybe years, away.

**LATE OCTOBER**

Half-bare trees shiver in a twilight sky;
a northern gale repeats its ghostly plea.
I stop to look as rebel daydreams flee
with ordered thoughts. So very hard I try
to stage with words the wondrous magic my
mind crafts, but I delete the words I see.
My iPod sings a truer poetry.
I turn back to a blank screen with a sigh.
The room returns—too messy, too lived-in—
much like my life now youth and dreams are gone.
I struggle to my feet and stumble on
as chimes from both grandfather clocks begin.
My bed I find and soon lie down upon.
I lie there while the long night closes in.

## PUPPY AT THE ANIMAL SHELTER

With boisterous barking
and longing leaps
and big brown eyes filled with hope,

he pleads to be

scampering across our lush lawns,
trampling through our prize-winning flowers,
digging beneath our majestic maple trees,
and chasing after our plump and pretentious felines.

But, as we hurry by,

his cries fall on indifferent concrete,
and his warm soft nose presses
against cold hard steel.

## TRASH

Trash has spread across the landscape
like political correctness and neo-fascism across the culture.
The North is overrun with trash. So is the South.
The East has it piled high. So does the West.
The oceans are drowning in trash. So is politics. And academia. And media.
*That boy/girl can talk some trash. He/She must be an expert.*
For the real experts, talk to your neighborhood garbage collectors.
*These days we have to work triple shifts to pick up all the trash.*
*Some of that trash sure does smell, and not in a good way.*

The film *American Beauty* has a famous scene
of trash being blown back and forth by the wind,
a masterful cinematic moment. However, in reality
unlike the movies, trash is being blown all over the landscape
and, contrarians believe, the mindscape of our country
where someone will have to clean it up, if it gets cleaned up at all.
Unfortunately, my house has its share of trash. So does your house.
And the hoarder next door, well, you haven't seen trash until you go for a visit.
It's time to give some serious thought to clean-up crews and then get out of their way.

## HAIKUS, SECOND GROUPING

5.
Dark thunderheads form
above while sharp thorns impede
my pathway below.


6.
Humidity off
the chart, sultry summer days
prove so exhausting.


7.
A November wind
blows and stunning beauty falls
to a quiet death.


8.
January winds
come whipping across the Bay.
Many feel their sting.

## SNAPSHOTS OF MY FATHER, NUMBER 3

"Stop!" my father screamed as I ran
toward the highway that separated
our house and the minimart, the supreme
fascination for a six-year-old.

Although I saw no cars in either direction,
something about his voice, its desperation
perhaps, made me stop as a car flashed by.
It had come from a blind spot on my right.

Rushing to me from behind, my father wrapped
his arms around me as I turned. This former
Marine, who saw combat in the South Pacific
during World War II, was visibly shaking.

"Promise me to never cross the highway
without an adult holding your hand,"
he said as several small tears slid down
his face. "Promise me!" I promised.

That was one of the few times in my life
I saw my father cry. The next day he started
on one of his drinking binges, something I saw
as often as a black moon rising in an even blacker sky.

**VISITING A LONGTIME FRIEND**
*In memory of John Reveley, a fellow teacher and good friend*

Not long ago I visited a friend.
He was home from the hospital
for the second time in the last six
weeks. A hip injury from a fall
put him there the first time
and a blood infection the second.
He looked well, lying on the hospital
bed in the middle of his living room,
despite the three-day growth of his
beard and his eighty-two years.
"I feel great," he said, "but I can't
stand by myself or use a walker
because my legs tremble uncontrollably.
I'm a prisoner of this bed." He was
dependent on the home-care nurses
who like prison guards watched
over him 24/7. I offered my sympathy.
He added his doctor thought one
of his medications might be causing
his trembling legs. "So far he hasn't
found the culprit," my friend said.
Again, I offered my sympathy. Bad
luck often comes in a series of three,
I thought, wondering what's next?

The second round of the British Open
played on his TV. We talked about
how bad we were when we used
to play golf nearly thirty years ago.
You might say we were the anti-Jack
Nicklaus duo. We asked about each
other's families. You could tell
my friend still grieved for his wife
who had died four years earlier.
He kept glancing at an open letter
on the lamp table beside his bed.
"The home care company sent me
a bill for over nine thousand dollars,"
he complained. "I talked to them,
and they said my insurance company

would reimburse me as soon as
the paperwork was completed.
At the rate my physical therapy
is going, I'll be broke and homeless
before I'm well again." I now knew
what was next. I suggested he not
pay them until his insurance company
pays him. "If I do that," he said,
"what happens if the home care
company stops taking care of me?"
What a world we live in, I thought,
where so often there is a catch-22
even for old people in poor health.

Before I left, he told me the latest
dog joke from his younger brother:
*A talking dog walks into a bar
and asks the bartender for a drink.
The bartender says, "Why should
I give you a drink?" The dog
answers, "Because I'm a talking
dog." The bartender thinks about
this for a little bit and then says,
"Okay, go down the hallway
to your right. The bathroom is
the first door on the left."* I laughed.
After my laughter subsided, he said,
"It's a shame old people are treated
as badly as dogs." I agreed. I may
have added a maxim of my own about
the difficulties of old age. As I left I was
thinking the actual joke isn't on dog lovers.

## BAD KARMA

Bad karma sneaks up
on you like a pocket split
on a good bowler,
leaving you a little dazed
and wondering how
such a good throw could go wrong.

You know the saying,
what comes around goes around,
but with bad karma
what comes around keeps coming
around and around
like an obsessive stalker.

Bad karma blocks out
good karma like a total
solar eclipse the sun,
leaving you groping to find
your way while in
a sudden daytime darkness.

As the Twenty-First
Century dawns, bad karma
surrounds everything
from weather and money to
politics and our
fierce fondness for hate and war.

Bad karma needs some
bad karma of its own, wouldn't
you say? We should put
a hex on bad karma. Tell
it to go to hell! ...
But, maybe, it's already there.

# THE PROGNOSTICATOR'S VISION

everywhere i looked i saw
soldiers; i saw them in the maddening
jungles; i saw them in the fruitless valleys; i saw them
in the cruel deserts; i saw them in the brutal mountains; i saw them
on the chaotic seas; i saw the wars they fought—chaotic, brutal, cruel, fruitless,
and maddening; i heard the shrieks of combat jets as piercing to the ear as the thrust of
a razor-sharp bayonet to the flesh; i heard the explosions of homemade bombs as horrifying as
satan's laughter; i saw haunted eyes on faces as pale as the smoke rising from shattered
cities; i heard anguished cries from voices as broken and bitter as a family's grief;
i heard malcontents and madmen shouting *vengeance! vengeance!*
i saw the blinding lights; i saw the mushrooming clouds;
i heard the screaming billions; i saw the
ones i loved; i cried out; i—
!!!!!!!
!!!!!!!
!!!!!!!

but tell me ... who sees the emptiness? ... who hears the silence? ... who weeps?

# III. JUST A GLASS OF UNPREDICTABLE LIFE

## THE THING ABOUT LOVE

*What is love?* everybody asks. Some say
it's strong expressions of the way we feel
like writing sonnets that adore sweet Faye
or rugged Frank. Some say it's what we feel
like magnets pulling close for love, first sight.
Some say it's chemical since those unkind
sex hormones stir up wild desires tamed right.
Some say it's more the special bond we find
between a child and parent. . . . *I think not.*
It's love to teach your children how to skate.
It's love to rub your spouse's sore feet unsought.
It's love to work for them the jobs you hate.
Love isn't the feeling, lusting, or the wooing.
Love is in truth one thing: Love is the doing.

## PULLING WEEDS FROM THE CRACKS IN MY BRICK SIDEWALK

In early April,
after a heavy rain,

I spent an entire
afternoon pulling

weeds from the cracks
in my brick sidewalk.

I have my doubts
about how useful

this will be
since the weeds,

like my deep-rooted
sins, always return.

I have tried everything,
even toxic weed killers,

without success.
It might be months,

but the weeds
always return,

mocking my
foolish effort.

I use a trimmer
to hold them at bay,

but modern technology
can only do so much.

Since it is spring and
a time for a new start,

I ask for the strength

to make an exchange:

My weak faith will gain
the weeds' strong persistence

while my steadfast sins
will gain my many doubts.

**CUTTING BACK**

I cut the
overgrown
and
unwieldy
pyracantha
down to the
ground, but I
didn't dig up
the roots. Like
all my other
cutting back,
it returned
the next year,
as green
and
prickly
as ever.

## HAIKUS, THIRD GROUPING

9.
Mild days get severe
storms.  Fresh blossoms bring foul pests.
New green finds old aches.


10.
Standing alone in
a dull field of grass and weeds,
the oak never sighs.


11.
After gazing at
the stars, I turn back to the
rocky path I walk.


12.
Excited, Willie
claws and bites the catnip toy.
Ted watches and waits.

## SOMETHING UNEXPECTED

The attack was as sudden as a bad fall.
At first my husband said it felt like severe
indigestion, but the pain increased all night
and would not stop the next day. By late
afternoon we ended up in the emergency
room, where a doctor informed us it was
his gall bladder going bad.

He spent eight days in the hospital, five in
intensive care, where his arms had so many
IV's in them they looked like gigantic
pin cushions. He ran a mild fever and had
a small amount of fluid in his lungs. At
times he experienced shortness of breath
and double-you-over pain.

The doctors gave him a strong opioid
for the pain, which caused paranoia aimed
at the nurses. "They are trying to hurt me,"
he complained. Without delay the doctors
inserted a drain in his gall bladder to discharge
the foul stuff it was producing. Needless to say,
it was not a fun visit.

But this ordeal, like so many, created
something unexpected. My husband had
lost his appetite while in the hospital. Once
he returned home, it came back gradually.
At this point it was easy enough to make
some needed changes in his eating behavior.
A new approach was tried out.

He started eating three small meals a day
with more fruits and vegetables. He gave
up snacks after dinner and all soda drinks.
He battled like a pro baseball player not
to strikeout on sweets. He lost more than
20 pounds, and his pants now hang loose.
He looks better. He feels spry.

Seven weeks after his release from the

hospital, his gall bladder was removed
in an outpatient procedure. Two weeks
later my husband was back to normal,
but normal in a new and improved way.
It turned out to be one of the best Christmas
presents he ever received.

## SNEAKY SQUIRRELS

After my wife refilled the bird feeder on the maple tree in our backyard,
she told our grandson, who had helped, to watch out
for those sneaky squirrels because they would steal the birds' food.
I said, maybe, the squirrels are hungry, too.
Later, as we watched the birds eating from our sunroom,
my wife pointed out a sneaky squirrel
who joined in on the feast. The tag sneaky
stuck to any squirrel caught climbing our maple tree,
and soon to any squirrel at all.

If squirrels understood human language,
I wonder what they would think of the label *sneaky*
applied to their species. For that matter,
what would spiders think of *scary*,
rats of *repulsive*, and snakes of *deadly*.
Labels are strange and powerful things,
even more so if applied to the human species.
Think *loser, snitch, slut, racist, far right,* or *far left*.
Like one's weight, they are easy to gain but hard to lose.

## SNAPSHOTS OF MY FATHER, NUMBER 4

Late one Saturday night
during my teenage years
I banged open the front
door to our house. As I
did so, my sleeping father
jumped up, seeming
to literally levitate off
the living-room couch
as if he were part of some
magic act. He turned
with a crazed look in his
eyes as a maniacal "No!"
burst from his lips. That
look evaporated like
condensation on a warming
car window. He said, "Oh,
it's you." I replied, "I just
returned from hanging out
with some friends. You
must have awakened from
a bad dream." He looked
as if he were trying
to remember something
important but said nothing.
I went to bed, hoping he
didn't smell my beer breath.

Over the years I've always
asked myself what kind
of nightmare caused my
father to have that crazed
look in his eyes. Was it
a traumatic memory from
his combat days in the South
Pacific during World War II?
At the time this all happened
he was worried about his
small diner being burglarized.
Did this worry translate into
a nightmarish scenario? Sadly,
it is impossible to know what

demons torment another man
in his dreams, even if that man
happens to be your own father.

Later in his life, perhaps with help
from my mother's persistent prayers,
my father somehow summoned
the willpower to exorcise many
of those demons. As he grew older,
he stopped drinking, decided
to go back to church, and was
more at peace with himself
and the rest of the world. Today,
thirty-five years after his death,
as I try to exorcise the demons
that have a stranglehold on me,
I feel envious, wishing I were able
to find the strength to do what
he did. Although it is nearly half
a lifetime too late, I proudly
stand and salute you, dear father.

**WHAT MATTERS MOST**

The boy was crying near the front doorstep
of his home. He said to the old man standing
at a respectful distance, "It's not fair!
When my father died in Afghanistan,
everyone told me I had to be the man
of the house, that I had to watch over
and protect my mother." His voice rose
to almost a howl. "I failed to protect her
from this horrible disease. There's nothing
I can do to help her. I can't even see her!"

The old man, a neighbor and friend, bent down
to where his eyes were level with the boy's.
He removed his mask before he said, "You
know why you can't see her, don't you?"
"Yes," the boy replied, blue eyes glistening,
"so I won't catch the disease." For a heartbeat
the old man's brown eyes were glistening, too.
"Right," he said. "This disease is as easy
to give to somebody as a high five."
The old man paused before speaking again.

"Son, I know this is a tough thing to hear,
but we all fail at something every day
of our lives. I fail to finish writing
my book of short stories. A teacher fails
to inspire a student to learn. Even
.300 hitters in baseball, a sport
I know you like, make an out seven times
out of every ten at bat. Our failures
don't control who we are. What matters most
is we keep trying to succeed, *always*."

The boy stared at the old man, looking up enough
to notice above his white hair a harsh blue sky.

**Harold Whisman** is a 75-year-old poet who grew up in a small southwestern Virginia valley surrounded by the Appalachian Mountains. After graduating from Virginia Tech, he settled in Virginia Beach, Virginia, where he has lived for over 50 years.

He is a retired English and journalism teacher for neighboring Norfolk Schools. While teaching at Granby High School, he sponsored an award-winning high school newspaper, *The Spectator*. He has an M.A. in English and Writing from Old Dominion University.

In his "golden years" he enjoys providing after-school care for his grandchildren, bowling in two senior leagues, and writing poetry. He says all these pursuits at times can be frustrating but also very rewarding.

Having written poetry for several decades, Whisman takes his cue from Ted Kooser, who said that "a clear and accessible poem can be of use to an everyday reader." He wants his poems to be accessible and, hopefully, beneficial to all his readers.

His poems have been published in *Smoky Blue Literary and Arts Magazine, Ancient Paths, Your Daily Poem,* and several other publications. This is his first published book of poetry.

www.ingramcontent.com/pod-product-compliance
Lightning Source LLC
Chambersburg PA
CBHW030051100426
42734CB00038B/1216